This book belongs to

_____

Dedicated to the precious lives of babes whose first sight was the face of Jesus.

If you or someone you know has an Angel Baby, write their name on the line below in honor of their life.

_____

Today is a special day. Today, I the Lord have created...

a baby named

DAVID

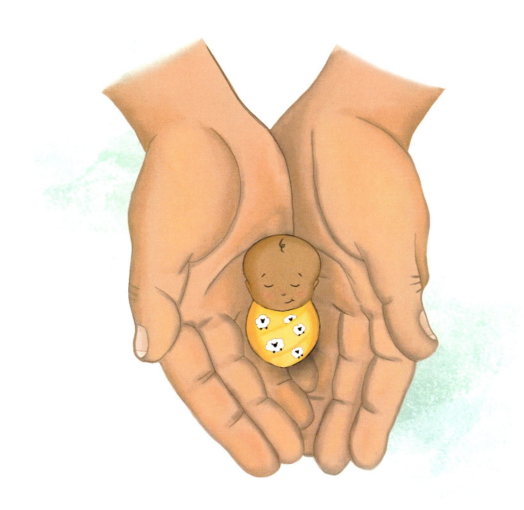

David may look small at first, but he is one who will do **BIG** things.

He shall be one to
LEAD.

1 Samuel 16:11

And He shall be one
to **PROTECT**.

1 Samuel 17:34-35

May He be **BRAVE**
and always
DEFEND MY NAME.

1 Samuel 17:40-50

His words shall be **POETIC** and his worship shall be **SOOTHING**.

1 Samuel 16:14-23

May his praise be **UNDIGNIFIED**.

2 Samuel 6:14-22

May he be **ANOINTED** for **GREATNESS** and a **CARRIER OF LEGACY**

1 Samuel 16:12-14 & Jeremiah 33:22

And Just as I, the Lord, have created David to be...

a LEADER

DEFENDER

UNDIGNIFIED WORSHIPER

and ANOINTED LEGACY

CARRIER...

So I have created

YOU!

Take a moment to pray over your child and write their name into the declaration on the next page.

Once you have done so, I encourage you to cut the declaration page out, frame it, and put it on display as a reminder of the destiny on your child's life.

I declare that

_____

will lead, with strength and courage.

Let no weapon that is formed against
them prosper.

May their praise be undignified and
their words carry weight and wisdom.

With every step they take, may they
be ordered by the Lord.

Let victory and praise flow from their
lips, even in the midst of sorrows.

And I declare that they are created on
purpose for a purpose, and will be one
to carry legacy and walk in an
anointing from heaven.

The Page of GRATITUDE

"Give HONOR to whom honor is due." Romans 13:7

Thank You Lord for entrusting a baby named Leah Grace into the hands of wonderful parents, Richard & Amy Kelley. They truly poured so much into me. I'm honored to have them.

Thank You for my siblings, Kalynn Jones & Rilee Kelley, who are more than just my big sister & little brother... they are my best friends.

Thank You for my shepherds and spiritual parents, Chris & Kristin Bartlett, for their leadership and the vital role they played in my walk with the Lord.

Thank You for my family, friends, and church, Bridge Church Boaz, who supported me through this process. And thank You for each business and individual that gave towards this book.

Thank You for Colin Edwards & his wife Lauren, for the gifts you have given them that helped make this book a reality.

And last but not least, Thank You for the individual reading this. Strategically, they have come into possession of this book and it is of no coincidence they have read it. May they never forget they are created on purpose, for purpose.

In the name of Christ Jesus, Amen

A Baby Named David
© 2023 by Leah Grace Kelley

Pictures and Illustrations/Courtesy of Leah Grace Kelley
Formatting and Publishing/Zion Media, LLC
ISBN 979-8-9888588-4-3, print
Printed in the United States of America
23 4 5 6 7 8 9 0 1

leahgrace.org (http://leahgrace.org)

Printed in the USA
CPSIA information can be obtained
at www.ICGtesting.com
LVRC100818130424
777227LV00013B/65

*9 7 9 8 9 8 8 8 5 8 8 4 3 *